# DAVID LONGSHAW

## INTRODUCES

**MAUDE**

**PERTINENCE**

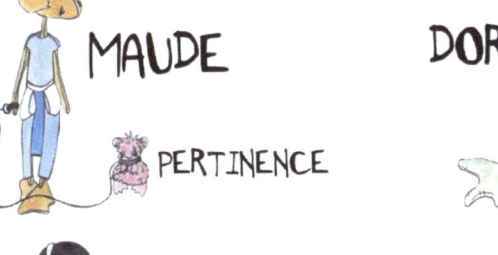

**DORIS**

**MILDRED**

**BRENDA**

**VERA**

**ETHEL**

**ALAN**

**MARTIN**

**THE PERCIES**

To see more of David's work — including fashion design, illustration and animation — go to:

## www.davidlongshaw.co.uk

I said to her, I said: 'Doris, **no!** You've got your own, stop trying to nick mine; you're always angling after what's mine. If it's not me Balenciaga hand bag, it's me David Longshaw dress, or me Chanel lipstick (I mean, who shares a lipstick? It's not hygienic!), and if it's not that, it's me Manolo's and more often than not it's me sodding sticky bun or scone!'

'Well...' Doris tried to interject.

'No, Missy, no interjections. You always do this!'

1

A fashionable

children's tale for

grown-ups

# For Mum and Dad

DAVID LONGSHAW
PRESENTS TO YOU,
THE MAUDE & DORIS SERIES
THE STORY OF MAUDE
(A fashionable children's tale for grown-ups.)
Written and illustrated by David Longshaw.

First    published in 2014
Text and illustrations copyright David Longshaw 2014
David Longshaw Ltd

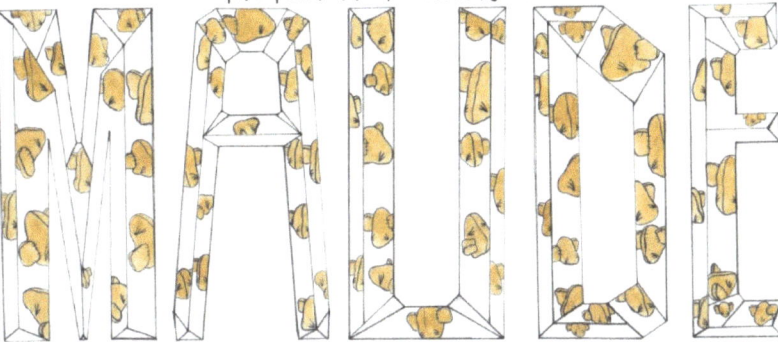

To see more of David's work - including fashion design, illustration and animation - go to:

# www.davidlongshaw.co.uk

MAUDE

To see more of David's work including fashion design, illustration and animation go to:

www.davidlongshaw.co.uk

I was talking to Doris (Co-founder and Director of Photography and Drinking for Maudezine) during one of our magazine meets.

I'm Maude, by the way. For those of you (the small minority) who are ignorant and unaware of me and my vast influence, I am Editor-in-Chief of **Maudezine**, the highly influential fashion bible.

I have appeared in everything from VOGUE and LOVE magazine,

EDITOR-IN-CHIEF

to the cover of the London Fashion Week's newspaper and even the famous **Saint Martins'** catwalk.

3

I'm a sort of fabric mouse (by sort of, I mean other than my colour and I suppose if you squint, my head and ears, I look sod all like a mouse, having scaled-down human proportions as I do). I measure 32cm in height and am made from 100% cashmere (the finest quality available, I'll have you know). But I'm sure you already knew all of that.

4

You know, I'm so successful I even have my
own stalker, he's called Martin. He seems
harmless enough; he's a hand puppet, so to be
honest there's not much he can do
on his own.

Anyway, I digress. The real reason I brought you here is to share with you my journey from fresh-faced fabric mouse to the influential fashion force and icon I am today, and my ongoing quest for the perfect home, a home of my own...

said Doris, taking a slurp from her vintage hip flask.

We started life as what I suppose you could call accessories. We were originally created to go in the hair and on the garments of a Saint Martins' graduate show collection (you don't get much more fashion than that). So from the very beginning, you see, fashion was in our blood, or more accurately, stuffing. We didn't have little wire skeletons as we do now (we had to get them made later), so we were rather floppy, but never the less we did the job with aplomb. Indeed, illustrations of me dressed in the collection won prizes.

8

said Doris in-between trying to make another play for my sticky bun.

'It was a struggle, though,' she continued. 'I mean, what with being only 32cm tall and made of fabric.

It doesn't matter how much of a visionary (like Maude) you are, or how successful a collection you've been a part of, height and fabrication hold you back,' said Doris sagely.

Doris was right. **We** knew we wanted to be in fashion, but we didn't know what avenue to take, and with the collection and show we were originally made for now over, I needed somewhere to live.

**I was on the shelf**, literally. I had been living there with the other accessories ever since the show had finished. But snuggling up at night to a pair of shoes on one side and another fabric mouse on the other was no sort of existence and it certainly wasn't conducive to a good night's sleep or contemplation of my future career path.

So, when an old sock drawer became available, I jumped at the chance.

Well, we all have to start somewhere on the property ladder — and this one even came with a pair of left-over socks, which doubled up nicely as a sleeping bag and pillow for someone of fabric-mouse size (just until I could sort out proper furniture, you understand). The trouble was, at the end of the day, when all's said and done, it was a sock drawer and there's nothing very fashionable about that. So once more it was time for a move.

**One** of the main problems about the drawer was that it was so obviously a drawer, not a house. Another was how claustrophobic it could get when it was shut. So I found myself a nice little shoebox instead. An odd choice you may think, but at least shoes are more fashion than socks, and with a bit of customising – namely cutting out a little door and some windows,

and drawing on the inside to make a trompe l'oeil-effect luxury apartment – it felt much more homely than that drawer ever would. Doris and some of my other little friends helped with all of that – they're really quite artistic, you know.

'**We** are!' chirped Doris, wolfing down another scone she'd just found after a rummage in her bag.

The **shoebox** was fine in principal and so once again I turned my attention to my future career. I began to think that maybe becoming a designer or journalist might be the avenue for me. I'd tried to go into buying, but being 32cm tall and fabric does make it hard to get a foot, or paw, in the door with companies, whereas I thought that perhaps with design or journalism no one would need to necessarily meet me. I could be like the designer Martin Margiela – no one even knows what he looks like, but the fash' pack all loved him.

**Despite** being, as I've previously mentioned on numerous occasions, only 32cm tall, a shoebox was still a tad too small.

I tried to add another box on top and even tried knocking through, but I just couldn't concentrate on my future career until my environment was conducive to clear creative thought.

In the meantime, the room I had my little box-house in had to be vacated, so I — with the rest of the fabric mice and other accessories — moved to the garage, along with my two-floor cardboard home.

My plans for fashion domination were big, and a cardboard box home was simply not going to cut it.

Scaled Maude model

I needed an upgrade, so I collected as much cardboard as I could and, after serious sketching, I drew up plans for my new home, my own fashion fortress. Doris, myself and what would become the Maudezine team got to work, cutting, pasting and sellotaping my little castle, complete with draw bridge.

**The castle** worked out a little better for me than my

previous abodes, and I started to write off to various designers and magazines for work. But with no formal training and a lack of being human, all I got were **rejection letters**.

Mauds cardboard box home

**Depressed** with the state of things and realising cardboard — no matter whether castle shaped or not — was still, at the end of the day, when all is said and done, cardboard

and not a suitable abode for a budding **creative force,**

I decided I needed yet another **new home.**

16

Brenda the fabric toad-frog (don't ask) said at the time:

You can move house, but you can't move away from yourself

To a certain extent I understood what she meant, but even so, I couldn't help thinking that in this case, a new home was precisely what the doctor ordered.

17

Then it came to me — it was obvious, you see. What I needed, what I'd yearned for, was a home that reflected me.

What I needed was a house shaped like
a dress.

"I'd come into existence to accessorise a dress; my past, present and future were all intrinsically embedded in fashion, there was no other option, was there, Doris?' 'That's right, Maude, but it couldn't be any old dress,' mused Doris, taking a slurp from yet another hip flask.

20

**NO,** Doris was right. This dress had to be a one-off and extra special for an extra-special mouse (me). We tried out quite a few scaled toiles (prototypes, to you) after doing hundreds and hundreds of sketches, but everything from satin, silk and linen to velvet and tweed just didn't feel right.

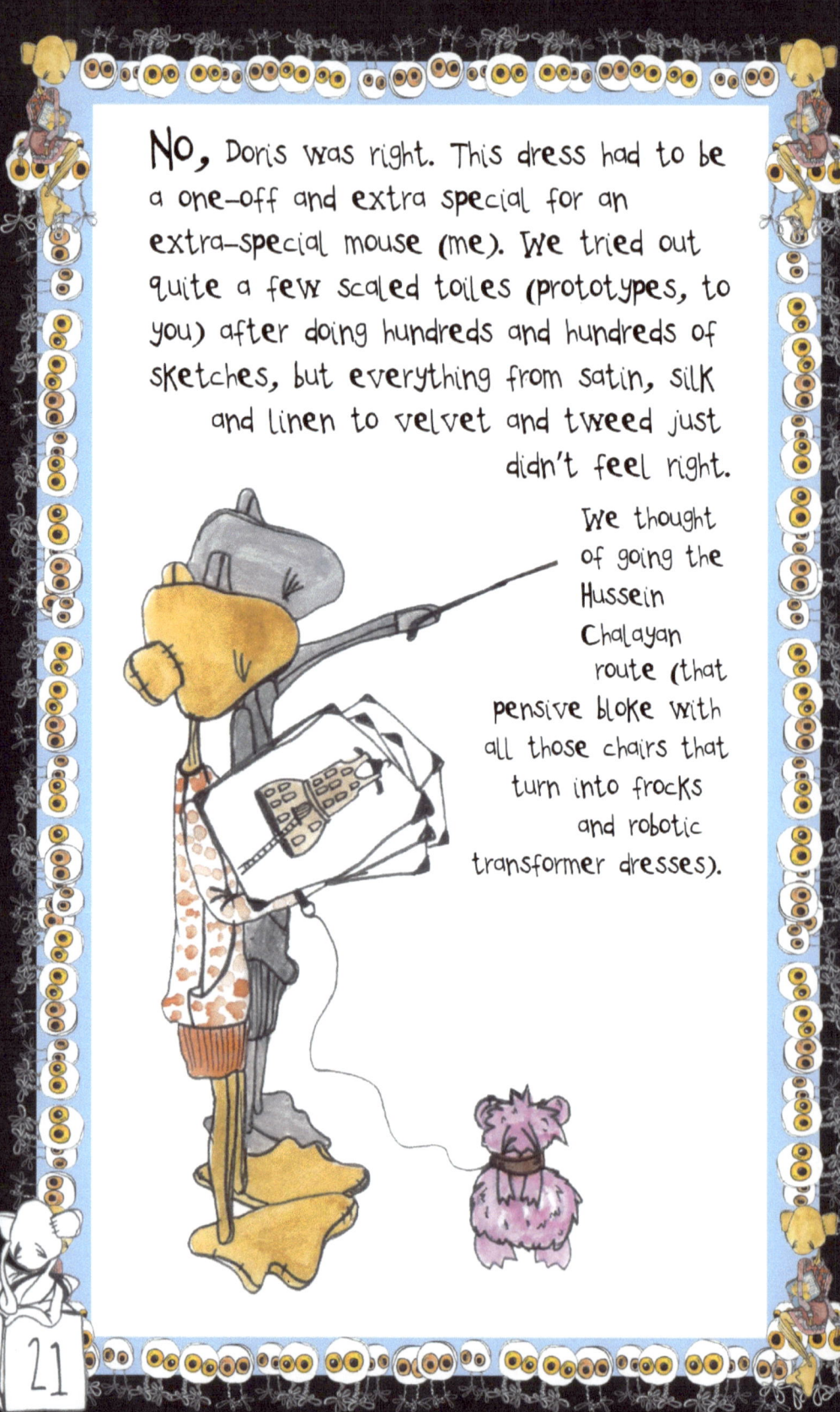

We thought of going the Hussein Chalayan route (that pensive bloke with all those chairs that turn into frocks and robotic transformer dresses).

We thought of being all arty and casting a
dress in resin or concrete, or sculpting it out
of marble, but nothing was quite right.

22

'They weren't, Maude, you're right. Even that rather fetching diamond and ruby-encrusted platinum armour one wasn't,' said Doris, shaking her head wisely and nibbling on some chocolate digestives she'd just found in her pocket.

You're right, Doris — that one was nice and it did serve some of the fundamentals of my needs, with it looking fabulous and unique,

' but it was perhaps a little ostentatious and less avant-garde than desired for a super-edgy, arty, fashion, creative thinker such as myself.'

Our budget was a little tighter in those days too, what with not yet being as fabulously successful as we now are.

But no more talk of budget, it upsets me so.

Creatives shouldn't have to think of such vile things – if Lagerfeld doesn't have to, why the hell should I?

AS with the notion of a dress as a house, the solution for which material to choose, when it presented itself, seemed obvious, like so many great ideas do when you finally come across them after going off on all sorts of completely random tangents. The thing was — well, is — that though fabric,

I am based on a mouse; when you think of a mouse (well, a happy mouse, not a terrified, dirty city one), you think of wide, open countryside; of it scurrying through forests and fields. What I needed was a fusion. A fusion just like me, of fashion and mouse. What I needed was a dress made of branches and twigs (beautifully made, of course — not just some twig house like a sodding animal would live in).

## It would be:

**1** At one with nature enough to satisfy my mousey side.

**2** In the shape of a dress to satisfy my fashion side.

**3** Suitably conceptual-looking enough to fulfil my pseudo intellectual 'aren't-I-edgy-and-unique-and-just-slightly-quirky-oh-I-really-am-at-the-forefront-of-modern-thinking-aren't-I-side', I also got extra points for this one because the house would be organic.

The design complete and intricate interior plans drawn up, we started construction, with what would become the Maudezine team all lending a hand.

Even Mildred, the peculiar penguin who sees people as dresses (don't ask), managed to help — though, as ever, she did get a little over excited at times, and we found her at one point trying to counsel a twig on how to find its inner dress, but I suppose that's just Mildred.

It was a real team effort, under brilliant leadership, even if I do say so myself.

Indeed, it was this project and the way we'd pulled together that made me realise that my future fashion success would be wrapped up in these little fabric oddities and their willingness to follow my every whim.

**It** must be admitted that I, like the others, had been having little success in the fashion system before this dress house, but now that I finally had a suitable home of my own and an initial base for the future projects, I set about planning.

I had dabbled in writing, in design, in photography and every other imaginable aspect of fashion, but no one would take a **32cm fabric mouse** seriously. So I thought, blow it

**If** I can't get into magazines, I'll bloody well create my own. And so assembling my disparate bunch of curious fabric creatures, each with their own peculiarity and idiosyncrasy, we founded the future fashion bible **that was and still is Maudezine.**

The title, though we played around with others, was in essence an obvious one — well, if it's good enough for Oprah to call hers Oprah, why not Maudezine?

# MAUDE zine

I mean, it's my magazine and you have to give the public what they want, namely me (they just didn't know it yet). It was perfect.

As Doris, my constant companion and over-partied sounding board, was a keen photographer (she'd been taking inspiration images for the dress-house project, as well as documenting the whole process, from initial design and modelling, to the final construction), she would be the Director of Photography.

**Vera** – the little mole who had been left with me as a baby when her mother disappeared (we don't talk about the mother – she was a bad'un) – was always there for me, running around, organising and chipping in with excellent suggestions,

so she would be my Junior Editorial and Style Assistant.

**Ethel** – another fabric mouse, who had been so useful with her vision of the project as a whole, as well as creating props and staging to give drama to my interior design – would be ideal for the Production Director's role. She could create fantastic sets for our photo-shoots.

PROP

33

**Brenda** the frog/toad would be the Make-up Artist for the photo-shoots and Beauty Director.

She was brilliant with a brush when painting my house and crucially always had her emergency make-up kit with her on the build, so that despite the hard work and sweat, we remained looking stylish and radiant, which was terribly motivating —

I mean, there's nothing worse for moral than trying to do something when not looking 100% chic.

34

**Alan the owl** was the most surprising on the build. He was like a sculptor weaving the branches and twigs together to create my home. So I thought he would be perfect for Hair Stylist for the photos and shows (I already had visions of some quite outrageous creations that Marie-Antoinette would have been jealous of).

35

The Percies (strange little round, big-eyed hopping things who can't speak, with wire chicken-like legs and feet) could, I thought, generally help out, like work-experience people do. Well, there's always lots of them hopping about and they were usually helpful-ish on the building of the dress

(at least when they weren't getting caught or trapped between the branches they were supposed to be weaving together).

That just left
Mildred, the peculiar
penguin who sees
people as dresses

I thought that for her I needed to create a special role, and though fashion magazines don't usually have Agony Aunts I felt we would make an exception.

She loved hearing other people's troubles, be it fashion related or more mundane matters like, 'Why are we here?' and 'What's the point of it all?'

(Which is obvious: to wear dresses). She would be good at offering advice, as it took her mind off her own predicament; she'd certainly experienced some confusing times – well, you would if you saw people as dresses, wouldn't you?

A home of my own.

41

There we were, the dream team, and to think it all started from something as banal as me trying to find a home, a home of my own.

Maudezine

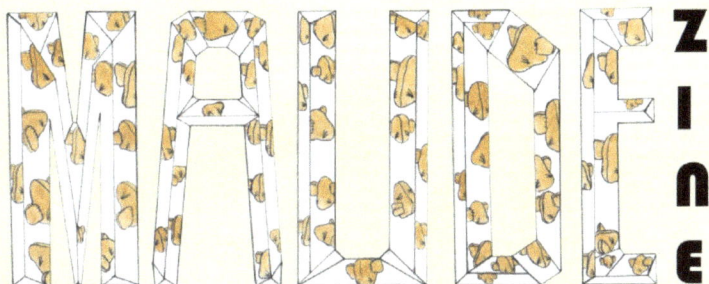

My personal quest for perfection in living set the
tone of the quest for perfection with our
Maudezine project. If it hadn't been for my
tireless drive, you may never have heard of me or
have experienced my genius. And that, my
Maudettes, would just not do at all.

I've been Maude and it's been your pleasure and
privilege to hear my story.

Maude xx

Maude
Editor-in-Chief
MAUDEZINE
and
Fashion Icon

MAUDEZINE, MAUDE STREET, LONDON, ENGLAND.

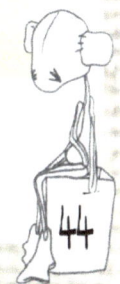

44

Team Maude ZINE by David Longshaw

46

Written
and
illustrated

by

David Longshaw

www.ingramcontent.com/pod-product-compliance
Lightning Source LLC
Chambersburg PA
CBHW050833290526
45792CB00001B/372